T0039781

MORE EASY CLASSICS TO MODERNS

Compiled and Edited by Denes Agay

It is easy to understand our pride in presenting Volume 27 in the Music for Millions Series, *More Easy Classics to Moderns*. It is a sequel to our previously published and now widely used Volume 17.

Because of the extended period of music history encompassed in both books, beginning pianists of all ages will discover material especially suited to their particular need. This material is easy enough to be used by the beginning student as his first sight reading book. At the university level, the student will find a rich source of reference to supplement his study of theory and composition.

The 148 easy, original compositions selected by Denes Agay involved extensive research covering the piano literature of more than three centuries. There is a wide representation of composers, including some of the lesser known masters, all of whom the player will be delighted to encounter. Some of these wonderful compositions have never been previously published in the United States.

All selections are in their original form, neither re-arranged nor simplified. They are set in approximately chronological order. Marks of phrasing and expression are often editorial additions, especially in the music of the pre-classic period. These signs were added for a quicker and easier understanding of the structure and mood of the compositions. They are to be considered as suggestions rather than right directions.

Students, teachers, and all pianists should find these original miniatures valuable for study, recital, sight reading, or just relaxing musical entertainment of the highest caliber.

Order No. AM41542
US International Standard Book Number: 978.0.8256.4027.8
UK International Standard Book Number: 0.7119.0408.1

Contact us:
Hal Leonard
7777 West Bluemound Road
Milwaukee, WI 53213
Email: info@halleonard.com

In Europe, contact:
Hal Leonard Europe Limited
42 Wigmore Street
Marylebone, London, W1U 2RN
Email: info@halleonardeurope.com

In Australia, contact:
Hal Leonard Australia Pty. Ltd.
4 Lentara Court
Cheltenham, Victoria, 3192 Australia
Email: info@halleonard.com.au

Amsco Publications

Contents

Song Tune

Henry Purcell
(1658~1695)

Dance Tune
（Borry）

Henry Purcell
（1658～1695）

Minuet

Andante

Henry Purcell
(1658–1695)

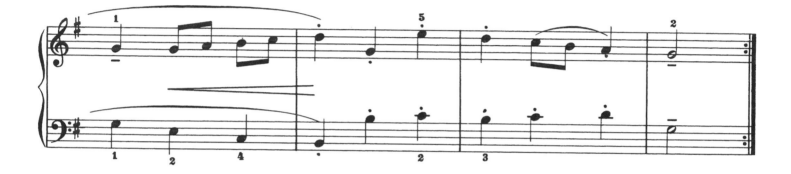

King William's March

Jeremiah Clarke
(1659~1707)

Old Polish Dance

"Chorea Simonis"

From the Organ Tablature
of Jean De Lublin
(around 1540)

Moderato

Pavana

Jan Pieter Sweelinck
(1562～1621)

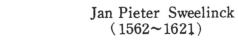

Adagio

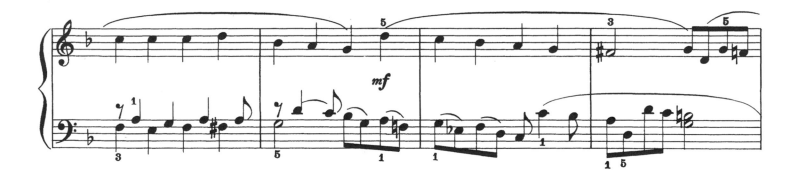

Fanfare Minuet

William Duncombe
(18th Century)

Moderato

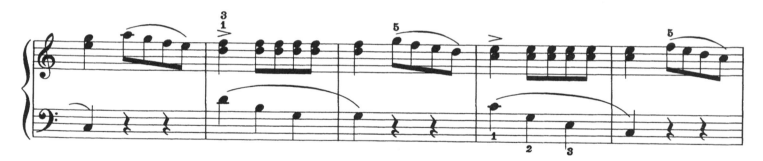

Hornpipe

Daniel Purcell
(1660~1717)

Prelude

Andantino

Henry Purcell
（1658〜1695）

Trumpet Piece

Moderato

Henry Purcell
（1658〜1695）

Largo

Arcangelo Corelli
(1653~1713)

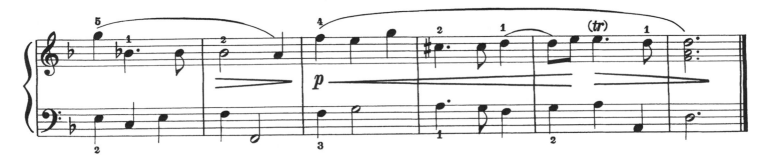

Ayre

Jeremiah Clarke
(1659~1707)

Allegretto

Arioso

Allessandro Scarlatti
(1659~1725)

Adagio

Minuetto Scherzando

Moderato

Allessandro Scarlatti
(1659～1725)

Fughetta

Johann Pachelbel
(1653~1706)

Allegro moderato

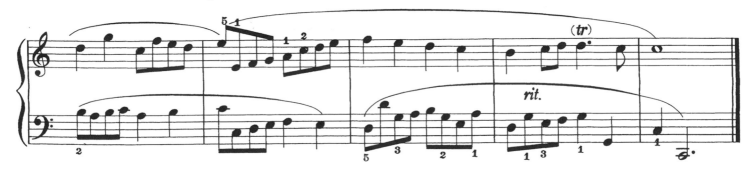

Gavotte and Variations

Johann Pachelbel
(1653~1706)

Var. I

Var. II. (Sarabande)
Andante

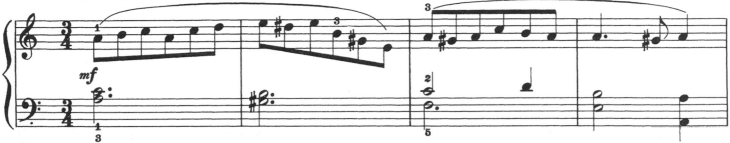

Larghetto

Domenico Scarlatti
(1685~1757)

Sarabande

Johann Jakob Froberger
(1616~1667)

Largo

Little Prelude

Domenico Zipoli
(1675~1726)

Allegro moderato

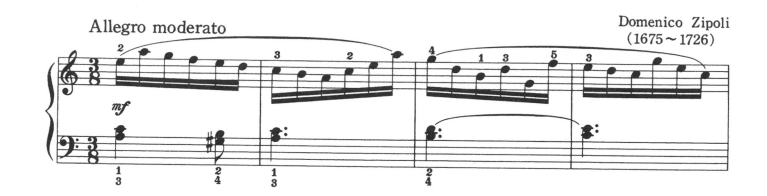

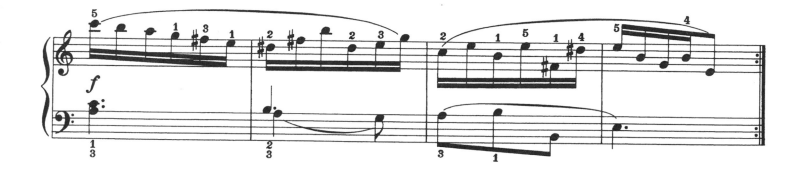

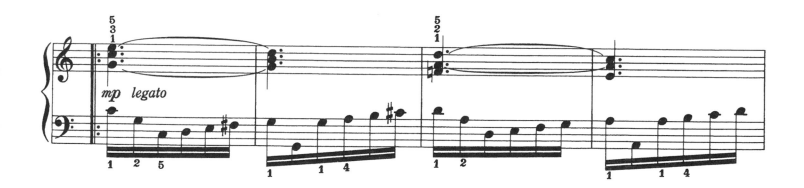

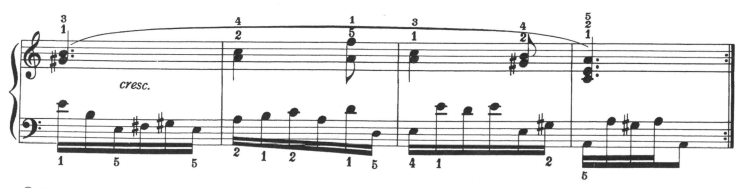

Little Fugue

Domenico Zipoli
(1675~1726)

Minuet

Jean Francois Dandrieu
(1689~1740)

Andantino

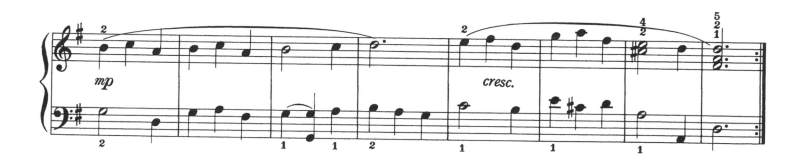
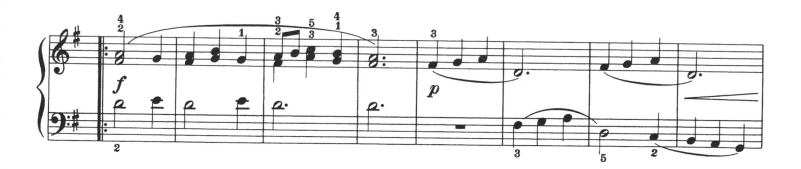
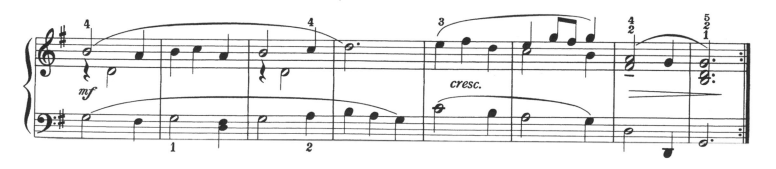

La Charolaise

François Couperin
(1668~1733)

Con moto

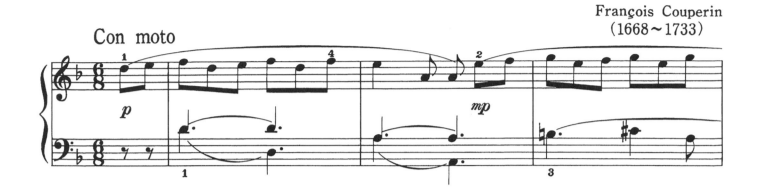

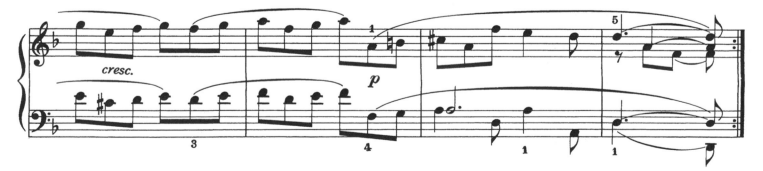

La Bourbonnaise

Gavotte

François Couperin
(1668～1733)

Andante grazioso

Adagio con Espressione

Sarabande

Johann Jakob de Neufville
(1684~1712)

Intrada

Christoph Graupner
(1683~1760)

The "Pipe" Aria

From the Notebook of
Anna Magdalena Bach
(1725)

Moderato

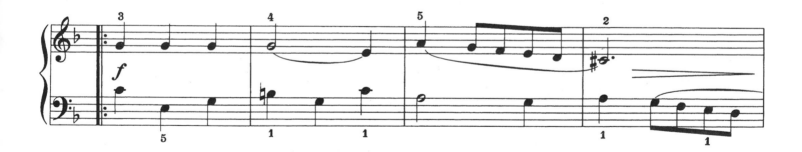

Gigue à l'Angloise

Georg Philipp Telemann
(1681~1767)

Minuet and Trio

Johann Sebastian Bach
(1685~1750)

Andante

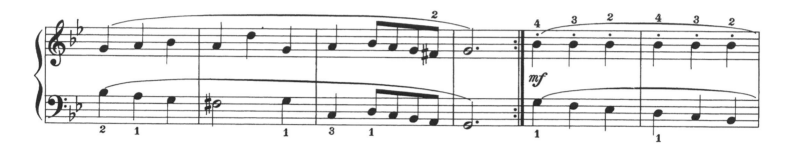

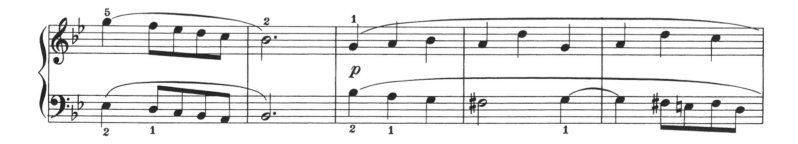

Trio
Allegretto

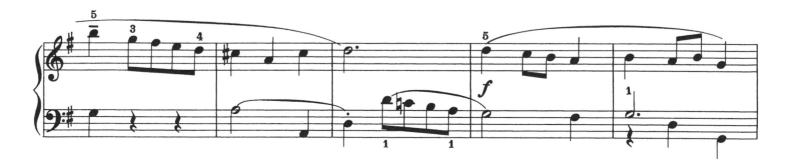

Minuet *D. C.*

Minuet in G

From the Notebook of
Anna Magdalena Bach
(1725)

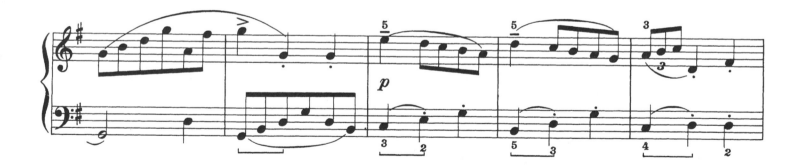

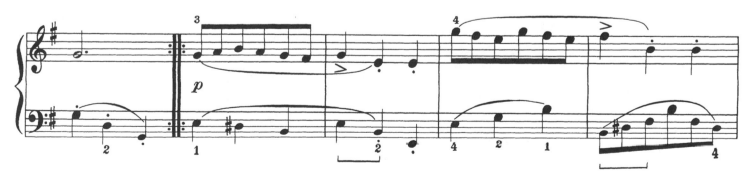

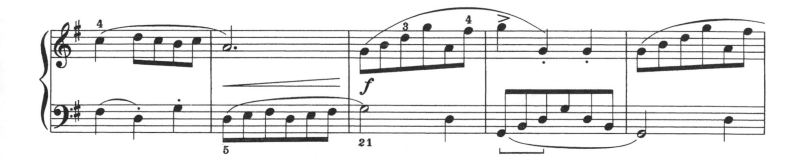

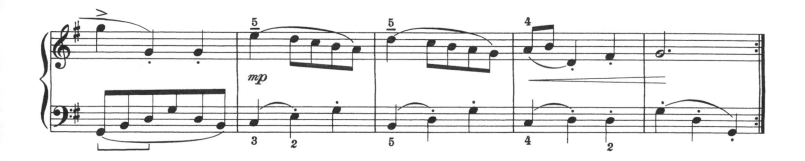

Minuet in C Minor

From the Notebook of
Anna Magdalena Bach
(1725)

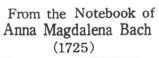

Larghetto

March

Allegretto giocoso

From the Notebook of
Anna Magdalena Bach
(1725)

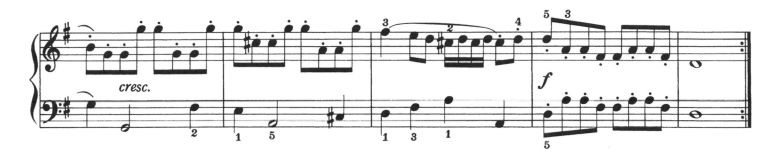

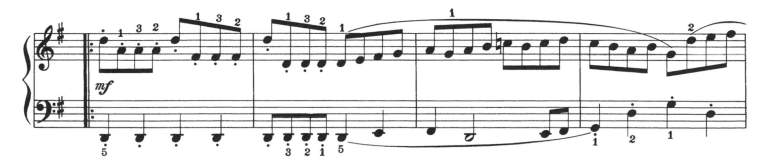

Aylesford Piece

Georg Friedrich Händel
（1685～1759）

Animato

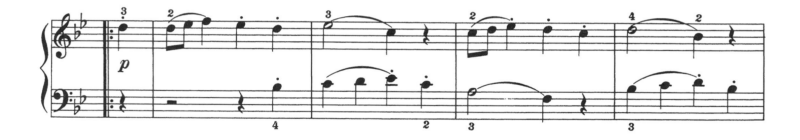

Rigaudon

Georg Friedrich Händel
(1685~1759)

Allegretto

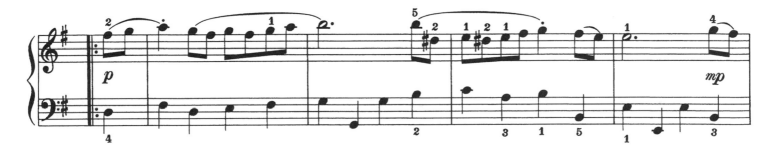

Sarabande

Georg Friedrich Händel
(1685~1759)

Lento

Andantino con Grazia

Georg Friedrich Händel
（1685~1759）

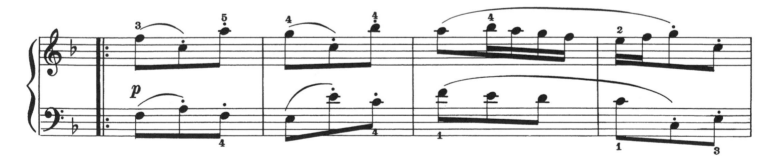

Bourrée

Georg Philipp Telemann
(1681~1767)

Allegro

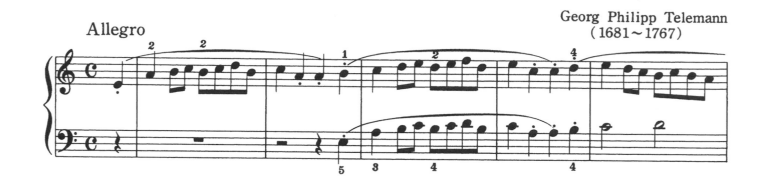

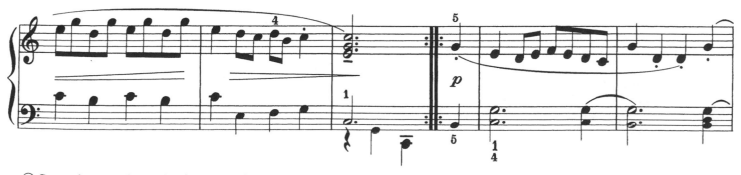

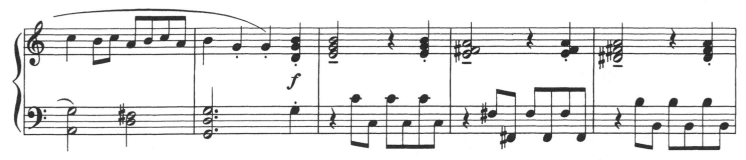

Tambourin

Allegretto giocoso
Theme

Louis-Claude Daquin
(1694~1772)

* The three sections of this piece **are** played in the following order:
Theme — 1.Couplet — Theme — 2.Couplet — Theme

Passepied

Georg Friedrich Händel
(1685~1759)

Rondino

Jean Philippe Rameau
(1683~1764)

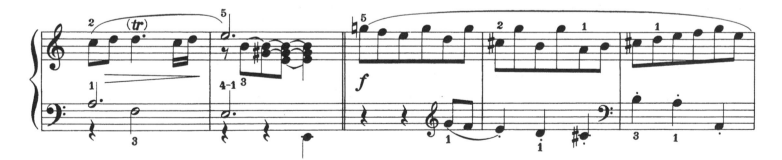

Aria

Georg Friedrich Händel
(1685~1759)

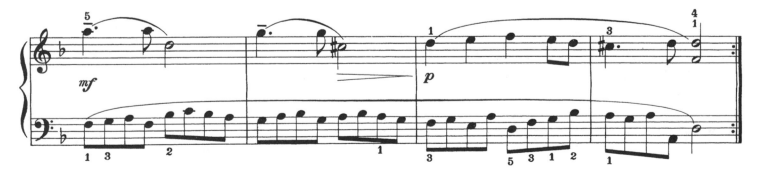

Pastorale

Andantino cantabile

Carl Philipp Emanuel Bach
(1714~1788)

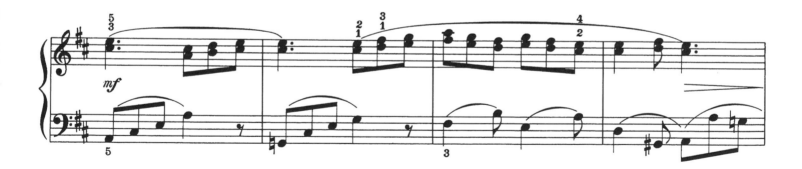

Burlesca

Wilhelm Friedemann Bach
(1710~1784)

Allegro moderato

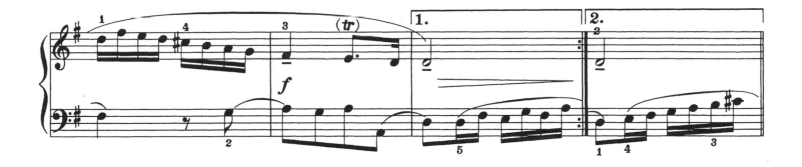

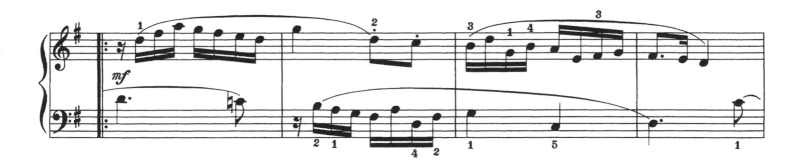

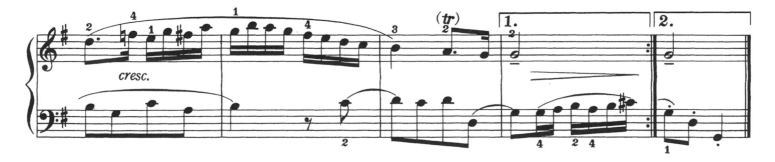

Lento Affettuoso

Carl Philipp Emanuel Bach
（1714~1788）

Lento non troppo

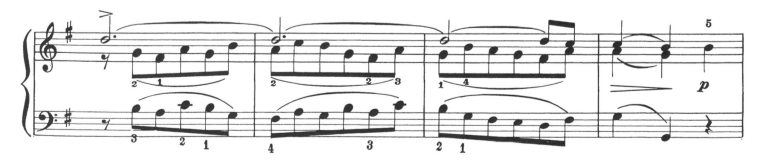

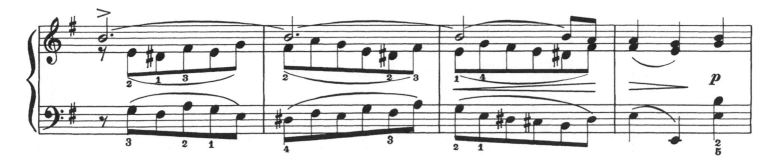

Schwaebisch
(Peasant Dance)

Johann Christoph Friedrich Bach
(1732~1795)

La Confession

Theme and two variations

Michel Corrette
(1709～1795)

Moderato

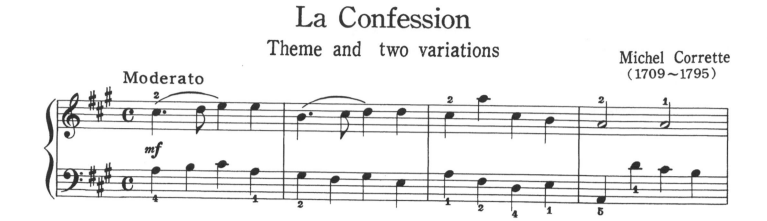

poco rit.

I. Variation

II Variation
Allegretto

Anglaise

Johann Christoph Friedrich Bach
(1732~1795)

Moderato

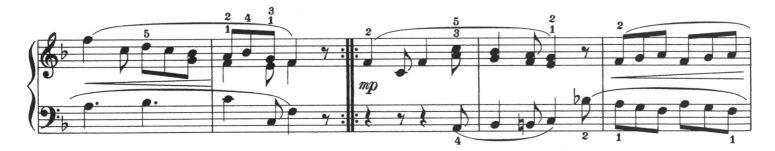

Old German Dance

Allegretto

Composer unknown
(Early 18th Century)

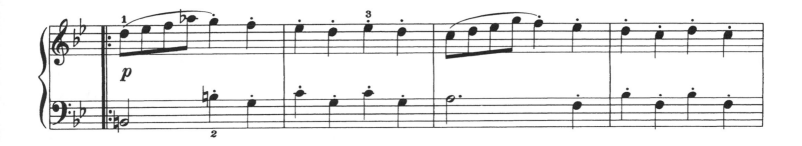

Polonaise

Christian Friedrich Schale
(1713~1800)

Lento moderato

Two Minuets

I.

From Leopold Mozart's
"Notebook For Nannerl"
(1759)

Allegretto

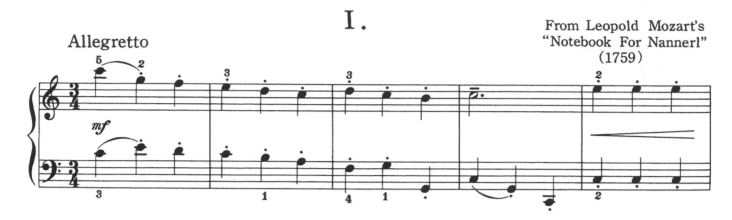

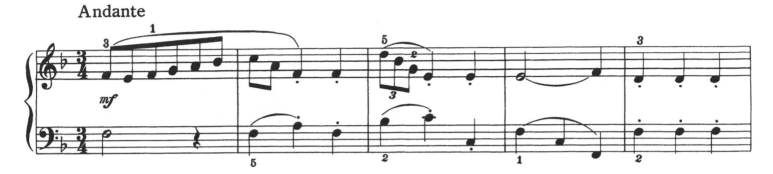

Minuet

From Leopold Mozart's
"Notebook for Wolfgang"
(1762)

Con moto; grazioso

Entrée

From Leopold Mozart's
"Notebook for Wolfgang"
(1762)

Allegretto

Balletto

Georg Simon Löhlein
(1727~1782)

Allegretto

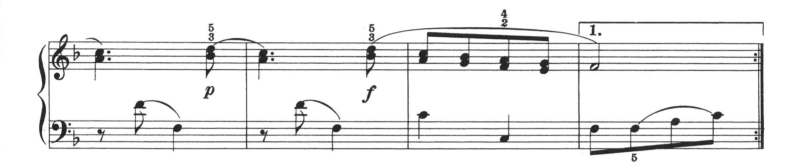

Les Tambourins

Johann Philipp Kirnberger
(1721~1783)

Allegro

Canzonet

Christian Gottlob Neefe
(1748~1798)

Allegretto Scherzando

Christian Gottlob Neefe
(1748~1798)

Country Waltz

Joseph Haydn
(1732~1809)

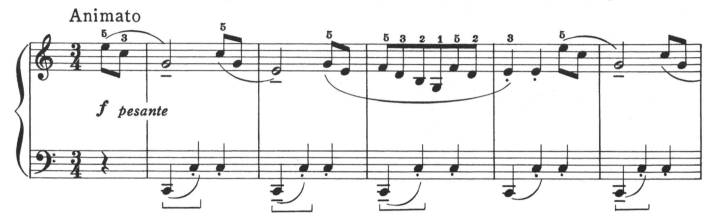

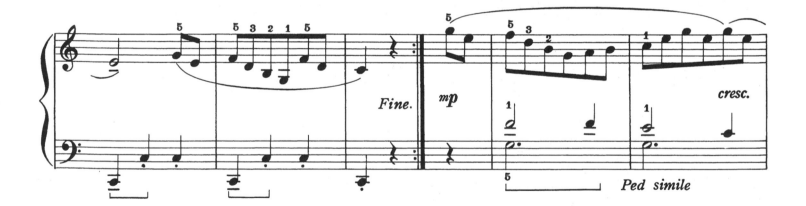

Gypsy Dance

Joseph Haydn
(1732～1809)

Allegro from Sonatina in G

Allegro moderato

Joseph Haydn
(1732~1809)

* Octaves in the original

Duettino

Wolfgang Amadeus Mozart
（1756～1791）

Andante

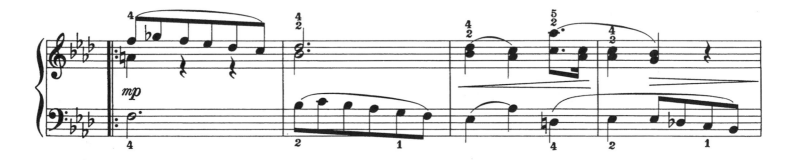

Country Minuet

Joseph Haydn
(1732~1809)

Allegretto

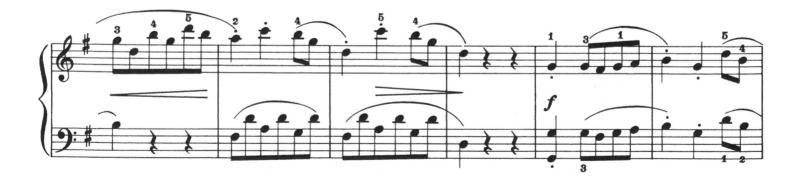

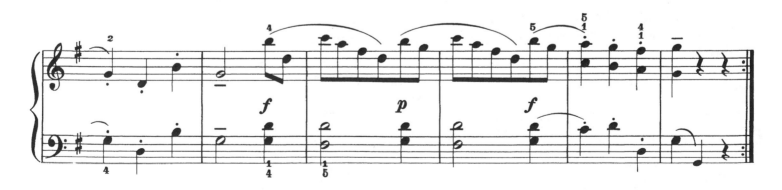

Andantino

Wolfgang Amadeus Mozart
(1756~1791)

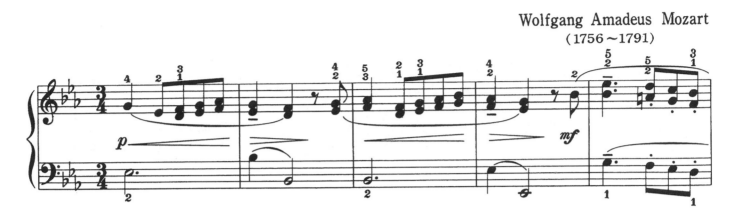

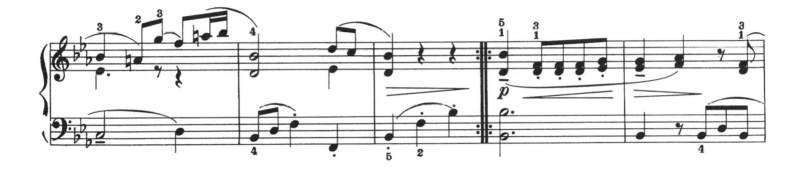

Contredance in G

Wolfgang Amadeus Mozart
(1756 ~ 1791)

Allegretto

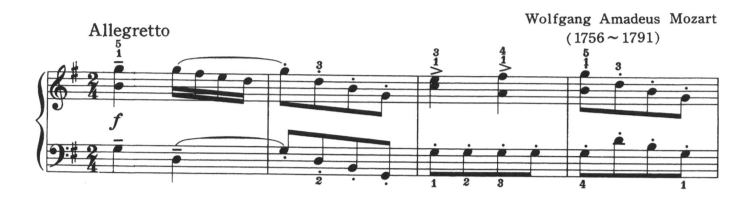

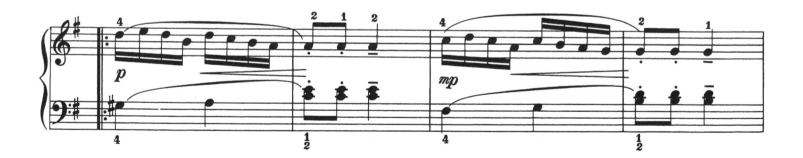

Contredance in A

Wolfgang Amadeus Mozart
(1756~1791)

Allegro

Capriccio

Johann Wilhelm Hässler
(1747~1822)

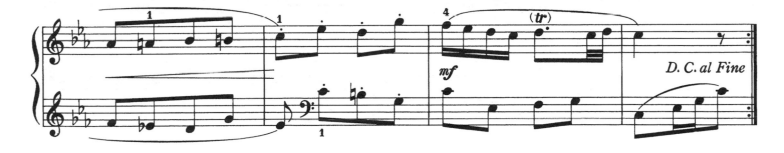

Gavotte

Johann Georg Witthauer
(1750~1802)

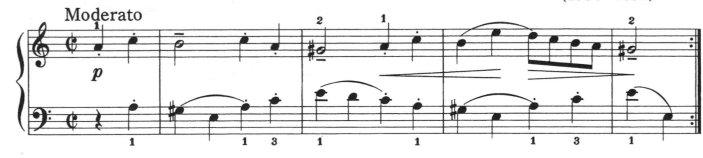

Children's Ballet

Daniel Gottlob Türk
(1756~1813)

Allegretto

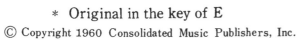

* Original in the key of E

Arietta

Daniel Gottlob Türk
(1756~1813)

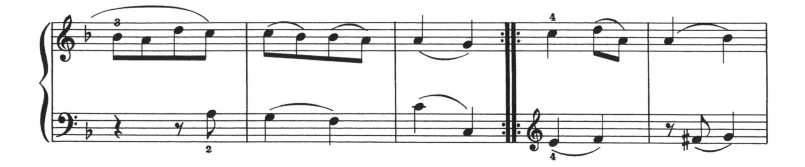

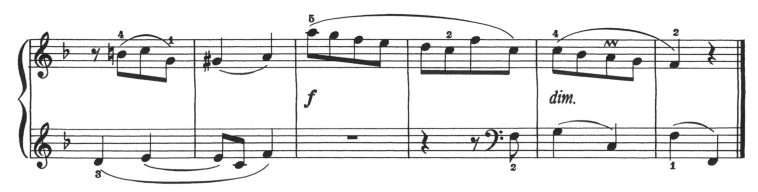

The Dancing Master

Daniel Gottlob Türk
(1756~1813)

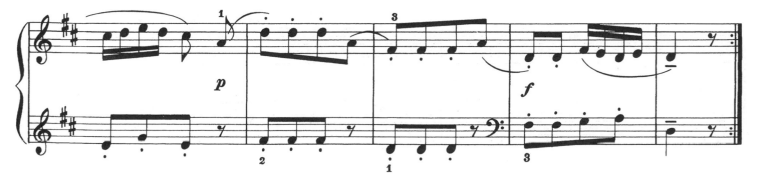

Scherzino

Johann Georg Witthauer
(1750~1802)

Allegretto

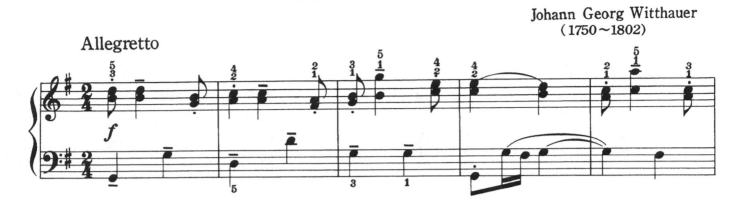

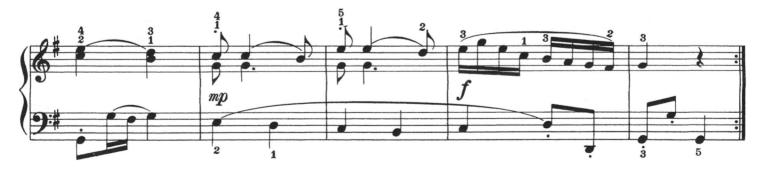

Rustic Dance

From Sonatina in D

James Hook
(1746~1827)

Allemande in G

Carl Maria von Weber
(1786~1826)

Allegretto

Trio

D.C. al Fine.

Air

Wolfgang Amadeus Mozart
(1756~1791)

Andantino

Theme and 3 Variations

("Ah! Vous Dirai-Je, Mamman")

Wolfgang Amadeus Mozart
(1756~1791)

Theme

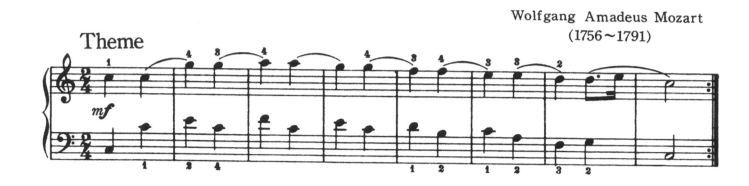

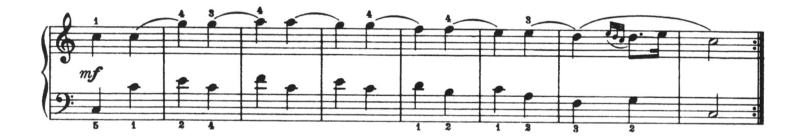

Var. 1

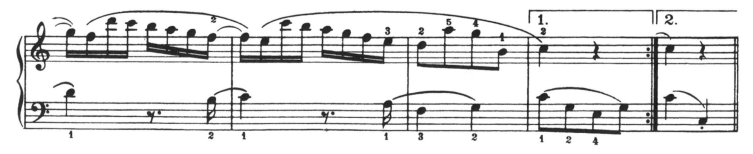

Var. 2

Var. 3

Ecossaise in E♭

Ludwig van Beethoven
(1770~1827)

Allegro Giocoso

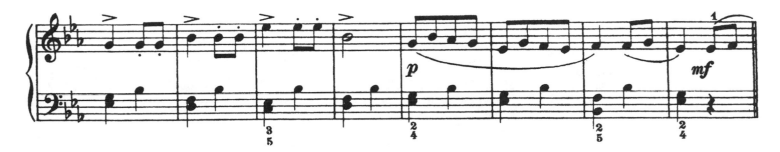

Six German Dances
I.

Ludwig van Beethoven
(1770~1827)

Allegretto

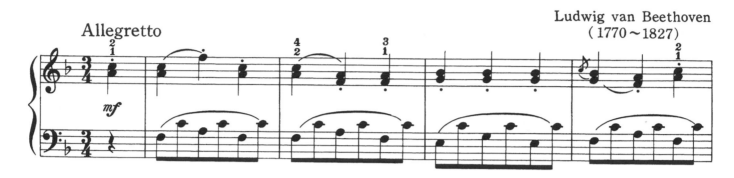

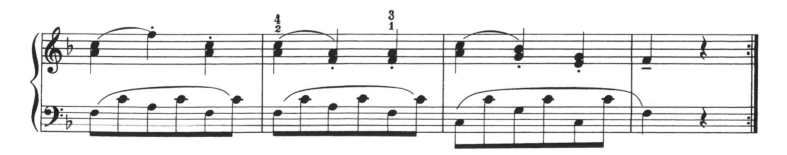

II.

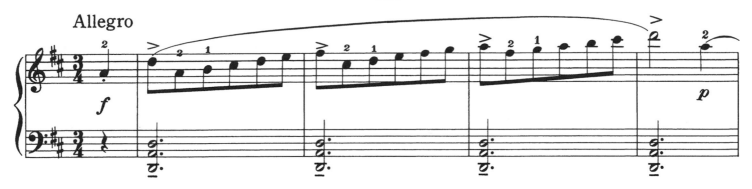

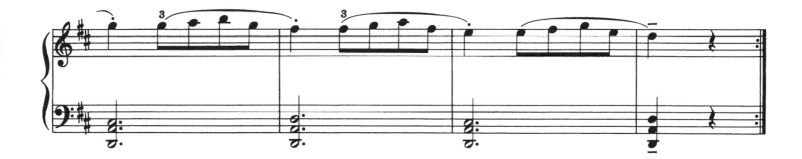

III.

Andantino

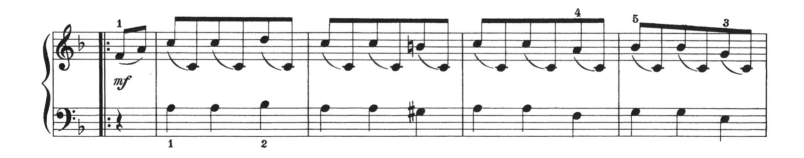

Trio

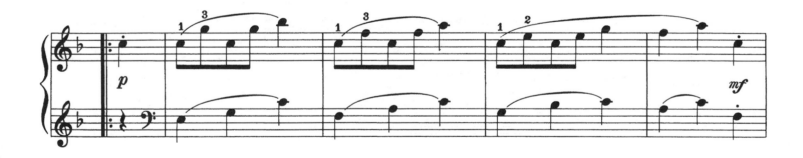

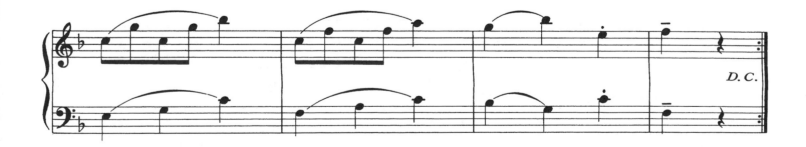

D. C.

IV.

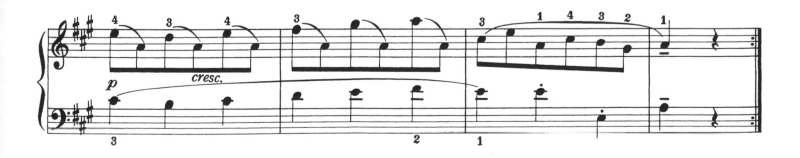

V.

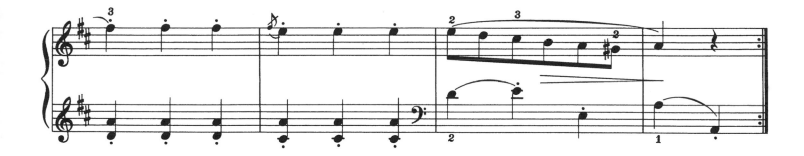

VI.

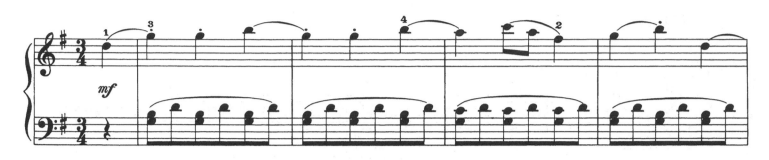

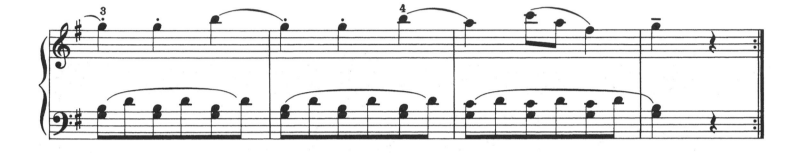

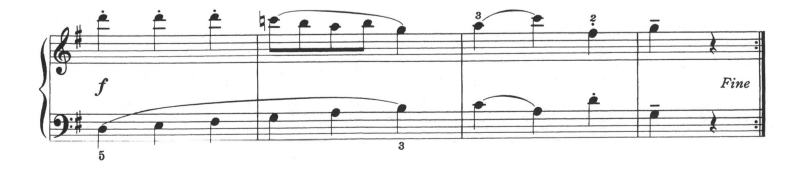

Trio

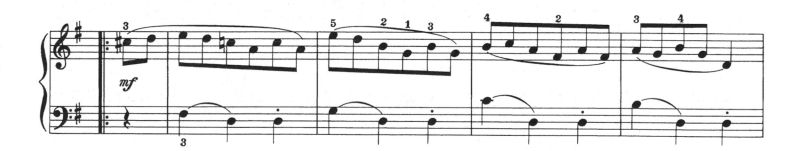

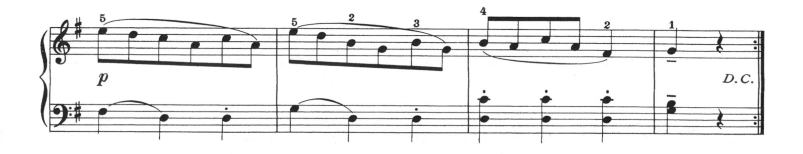

Allemande in E♭

Carl Maria von Weber
(1786~1826)

Andantino

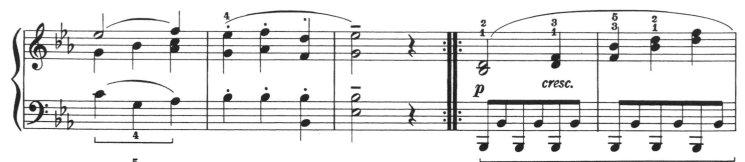

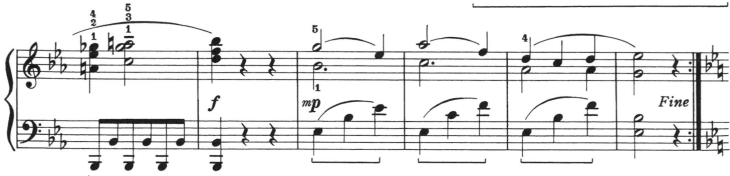

Trio

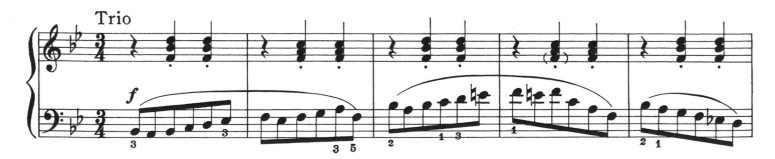

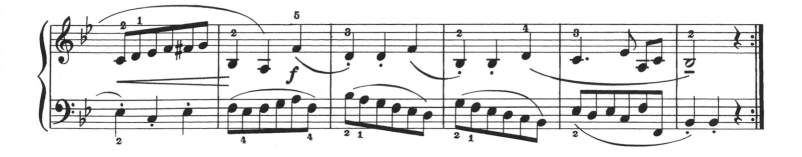

Walzer

Moderato; ben ritmo

Franz Schubert
(1797~1828)

Rondo in C

Anton André
(1775~1842)

Allegretto

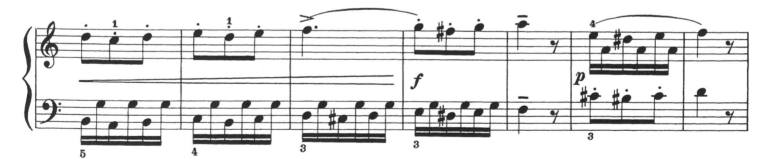

Air Russe

Johann Nepomuk Hummel
(1778~1837)

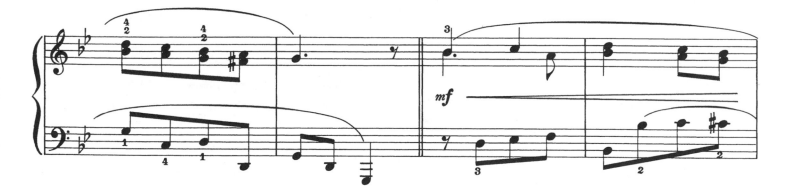

Serenade

August Eberhard Müller
(1767~1817)

Air de Dance

From Sonatina № 4

Jean Latour
(1766~1837)

Bagatelle

Antonio Diabelli
(1781～1858)

Andante in B♭

From Sonatina in F, № 3

Antonio Diabelli
(1781~1858)

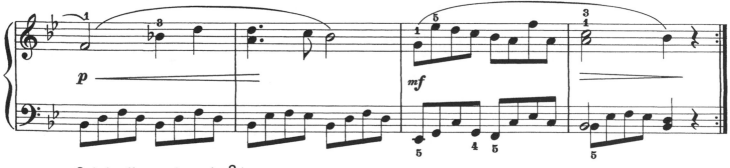

* Originally written in ²⁄₄

Sonatina

Ludwig van Beethoven
(1770~1827)

Moderato

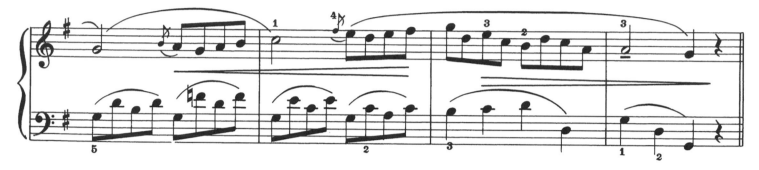

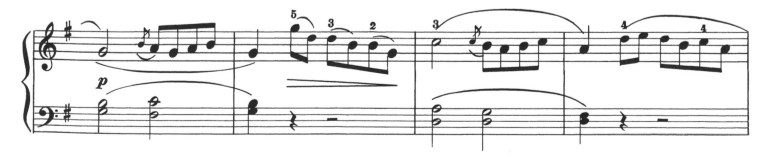

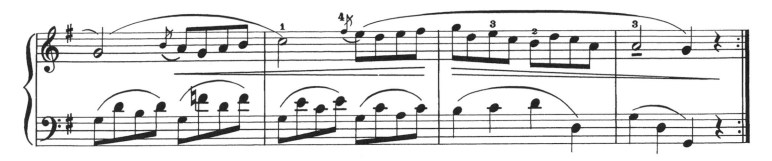

Allegretto

Bagatelle

Ludwig van Beethoven
(1770~1827)

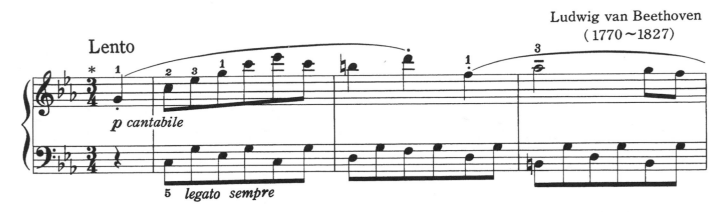

* Originally written in ⅜

Ländler

Franz Schubert
(1797~1828)

Moderato; ben ritmo

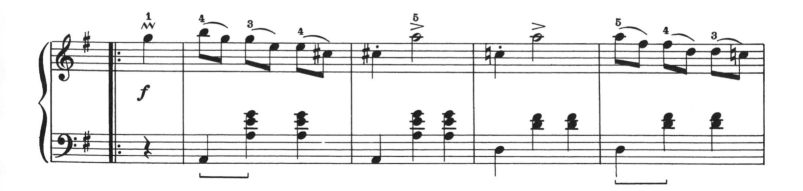

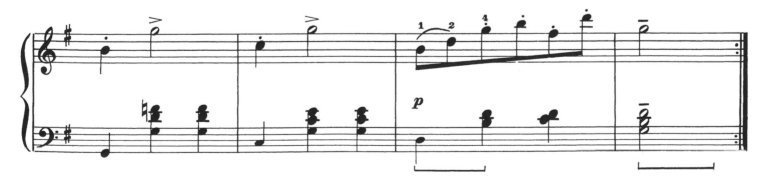

Two Ecossaises

I.

Franz Schubert
(1797~1828)

Allegretto

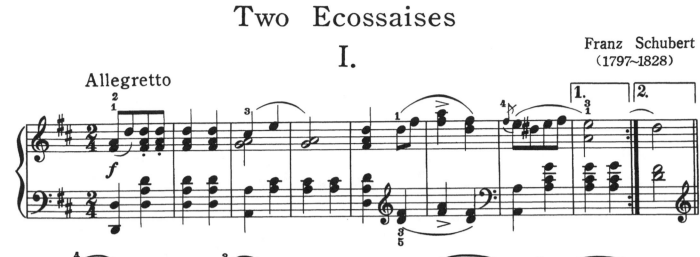

II.

Allegretto

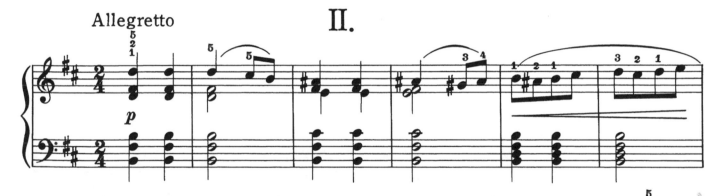

Choral

Robert Schumann
(1810~1856)

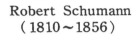

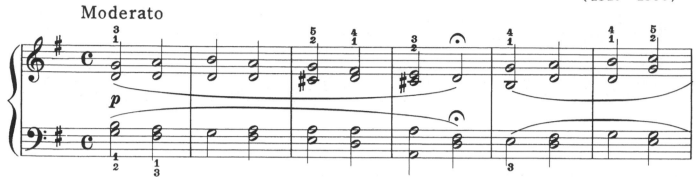

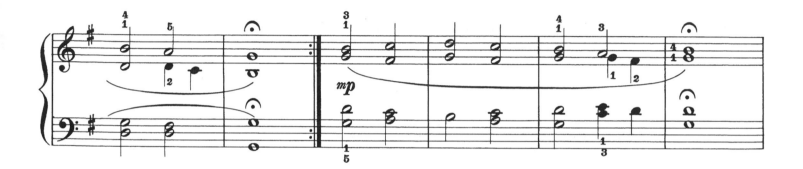

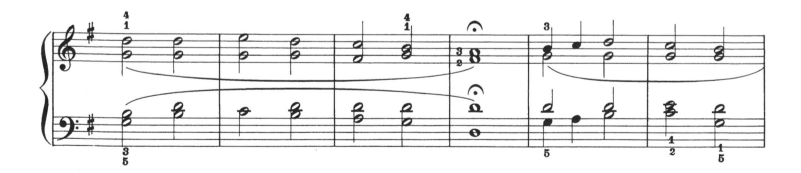

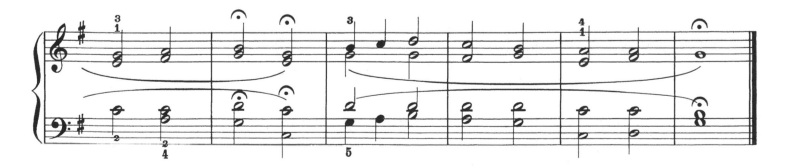

First Loss

Robert Schumann
(1810~1856)

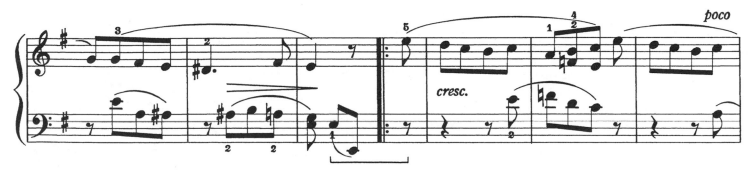

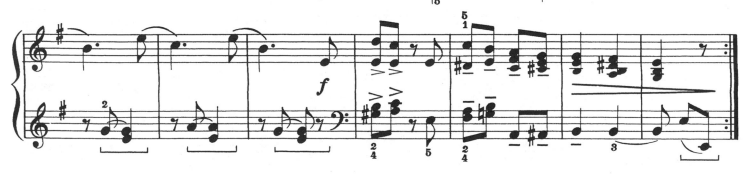

Little Study

Robert Schumann
(1810~1856)

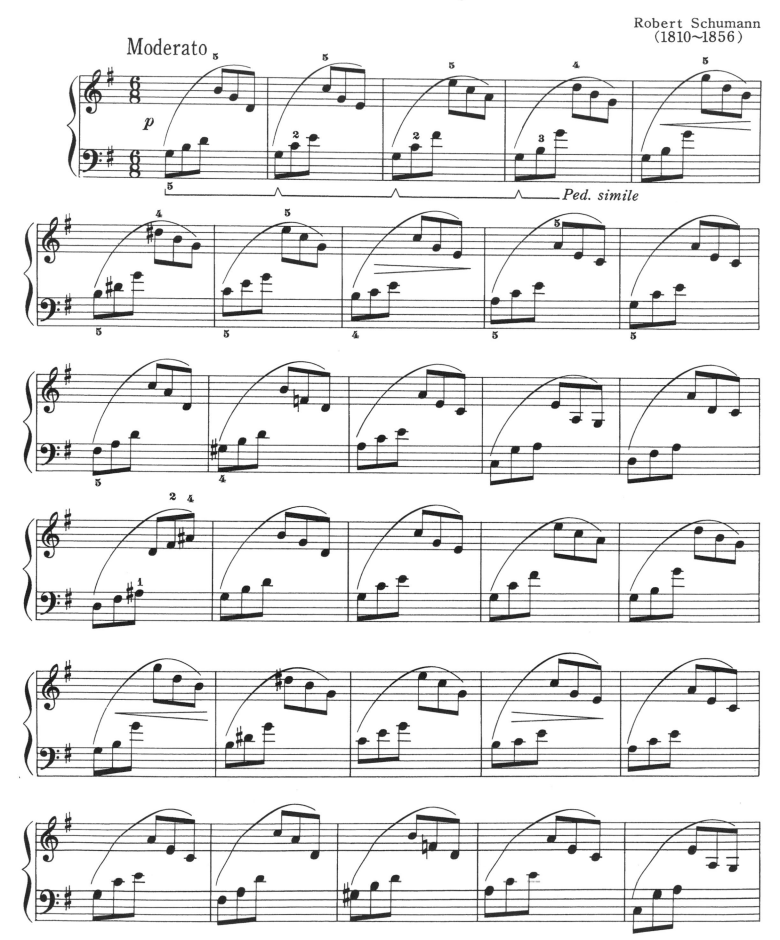

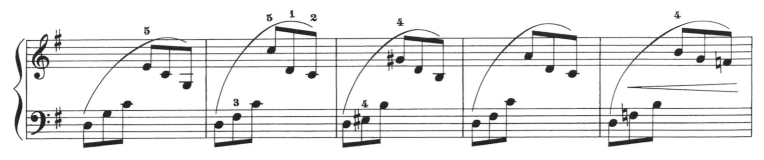

Ped. simile

Sicilienne

Robert Schumann
(1810-1856)

Allegretto

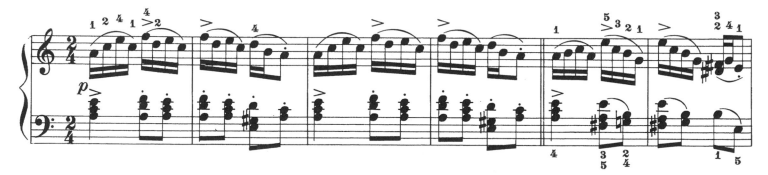

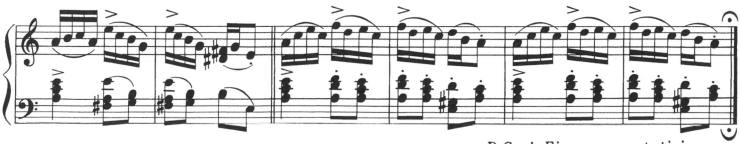

D.C. al Fine senza repetizione

Bagpipe Etude

Stephen Heller
(1813 - 1888)

Musette

Felix Le Couppey
(1811~1887)

Allegro

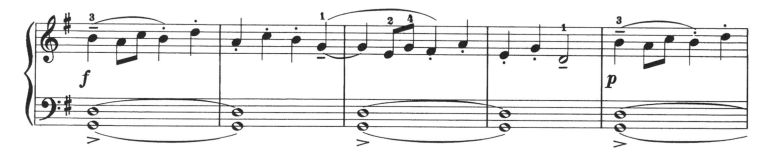

The Tale Begins

Robert Volkmann
(1815~1883)

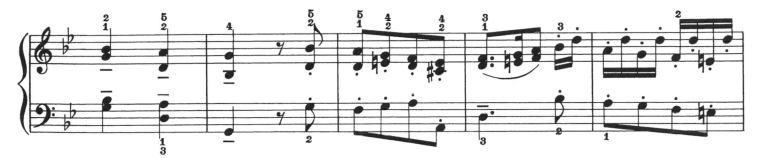

The Soldier's Story

Robert Volkmann
(1815~1883)

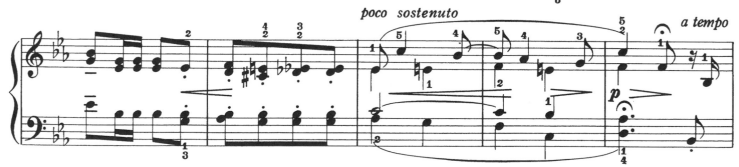

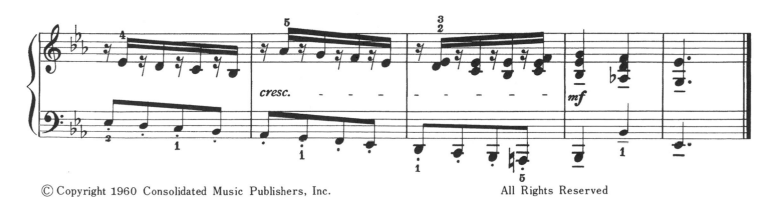

Intermezzo

Robert Volkmann
(1815~1883)

Lento espressivo

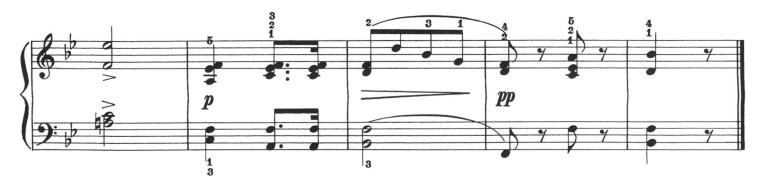

Postlude

Robert Volkmann
(1815~1883)

Allegro moderato

Two Austrian Folk Tunes
I.

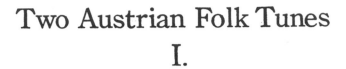

Louis Köhler
(1820~1886)

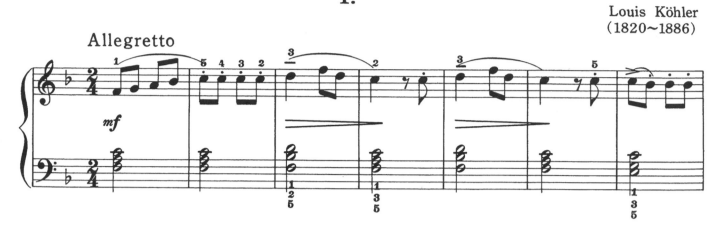

II.

Moderato

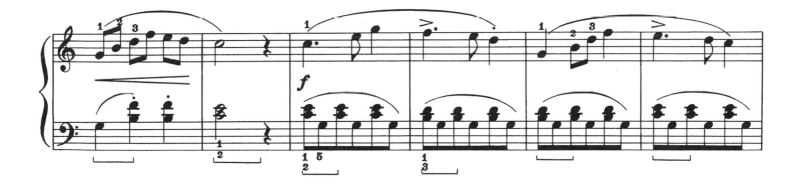

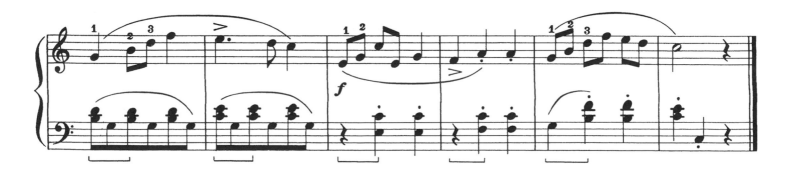

Russian Polka

Michael Ivanovich Glinka
(1804~1857)

Allegretto

sempre stacc.

Russian Song

Peter Ilyich Tchaikovsky
(1840~1893)

Con moto

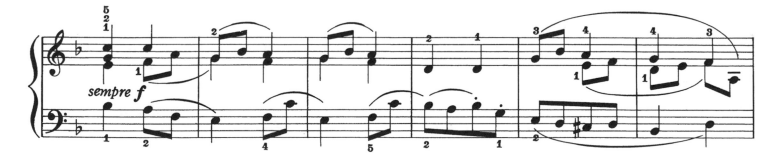

Mazurka

Peter Ilyich Tchaikovsky
(1840～1893)

Tempo di Mazurka

In Church

Peter Ilyich Tchaikovsky
(1840~1893)

Moderato

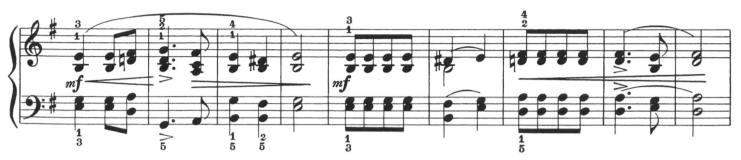

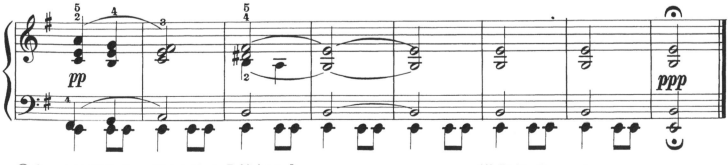

Christmas Carol from Anjou

César Franck
(1822~1890)

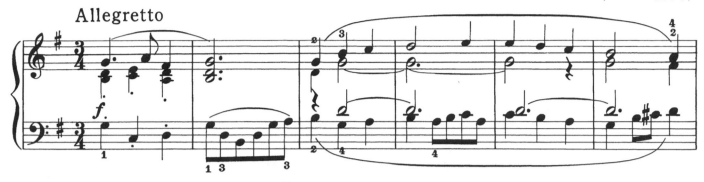

The Bear

Vladimir Rebikoff
(1866~1920)

Andante pesante

Folk Tune Scherzo

Theodor Kirchner
(1823~1903)

Allegretto

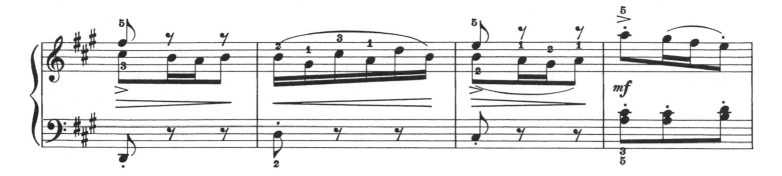

Lullaby

Hugo Wolf
(1860~1903)

Andantino

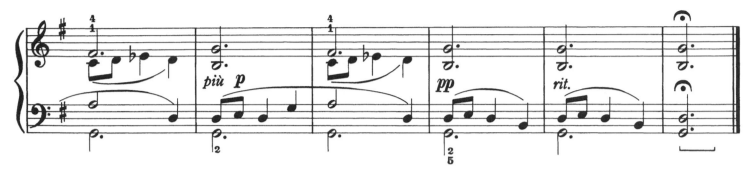

Musical Moment

Nicolas Miaskovsky
(1881~1950)

Andantino

The Chinese Doll

Vladimir Rebikoff
(1866~1920)

Allegretto

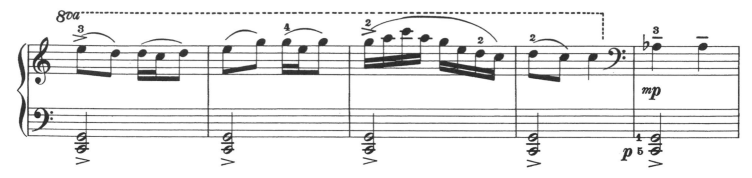

The Shepherd's Flute

Samuel Maykapar
(1867~1938)

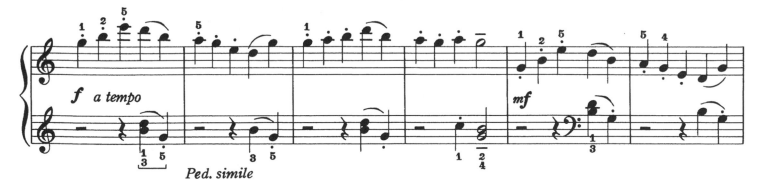

The Little Music Box

Samuel Maykapar
(1867~1938)

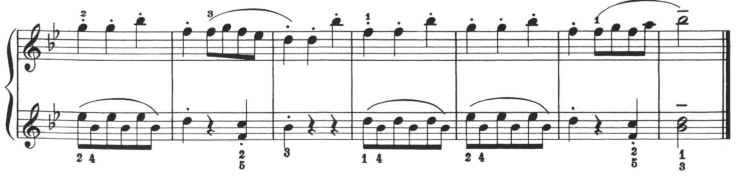

On the Swing

Alexander Gretchaninoff
（1864～1956）

Moderato

Autumn Chant

Alexander Gretchaninoff
(1864~1956)

Andante

Bicycle Ride

Allegro grazioso

Alexander Gretchaninoff

Around the Campfire

Eduard Poldini
(1869~1957)

Hopak

Allegro moderato

Alexander Goedicke
(1877~   )

Valsette

Rhené - Baton
(1879~1940)

Tempo di Valse moderato

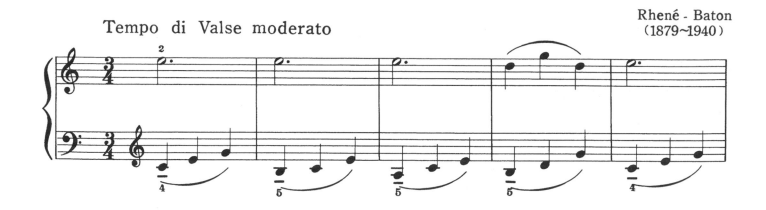

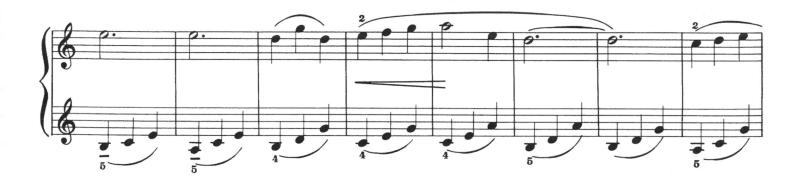

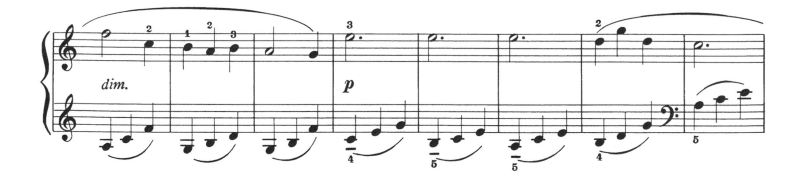

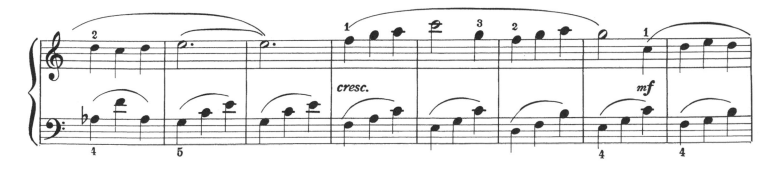

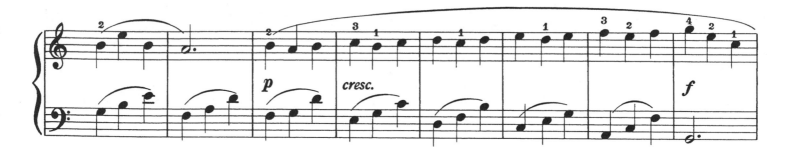

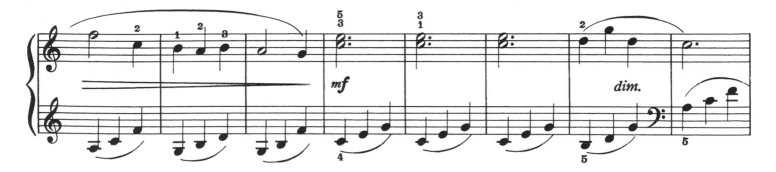

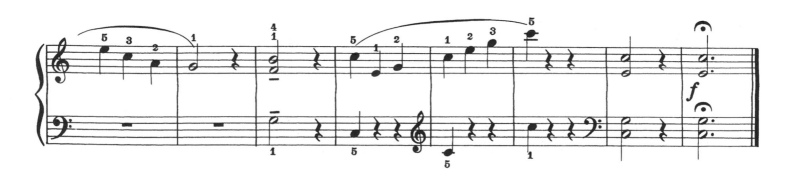

Chanson

Rhené - Baton
(1879~1940)

Moderato

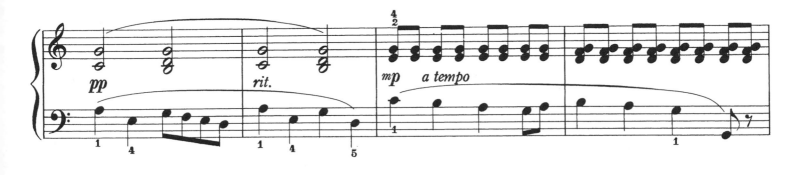

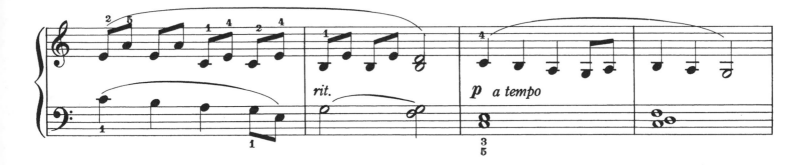

Five Finger Toccata

Igor Stravinsky
（1882～ ）

Allegro marziale

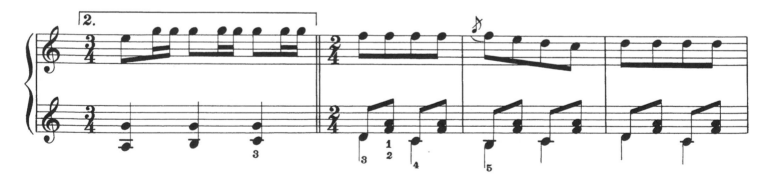

Waltz

Dmitri Shostakovich
（1906~ ）

Tempo di Valse

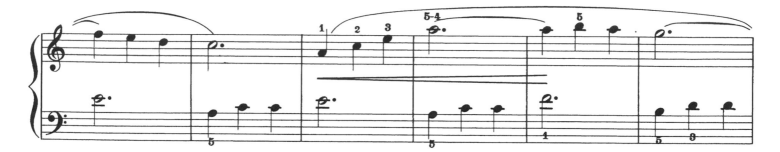

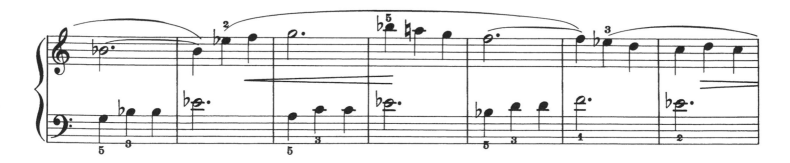

March

Dmitri Shostakovich
(1906~)

Tempo di Marcia

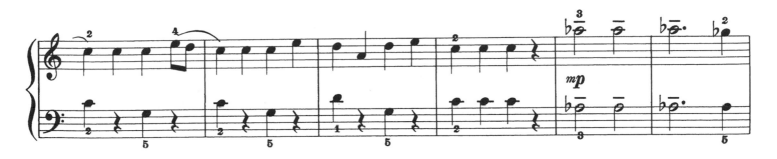

Dialogue

Nicolas Miaskovsky
(1881~1950)

Little Song

Dmitri Kabalevsky
(1904~   )

Little Scherzo

Dmitri Kabalevsky
（1904~　　）

Game

Dmitri Kabalevsky
(1904~   )

Allegretto

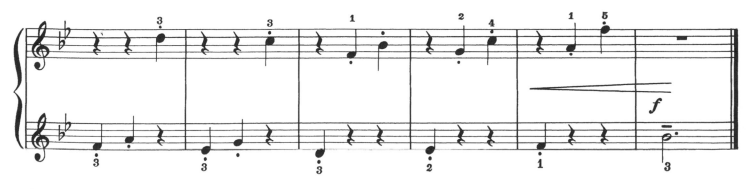

Folk Dance

Dmitri Kabalevsky
（1904～　　）

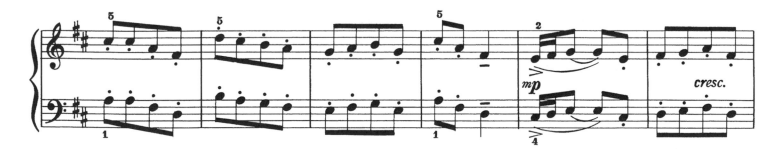

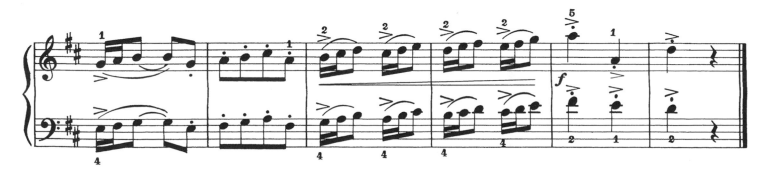

Waltz Intermezzo

Dmitri Kabalevsky
（1904～　）

Soliloquy

from "For Children"

Béla Bartók
(1881~1945)

Parlando

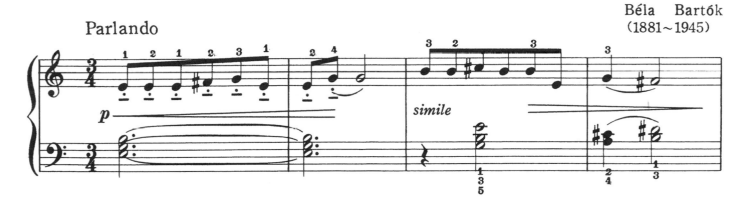

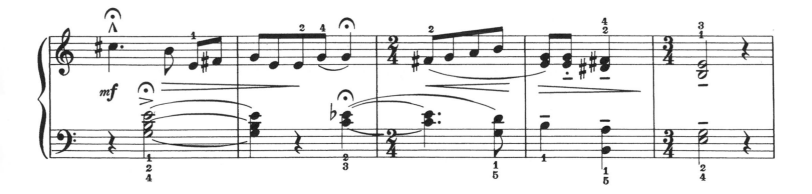

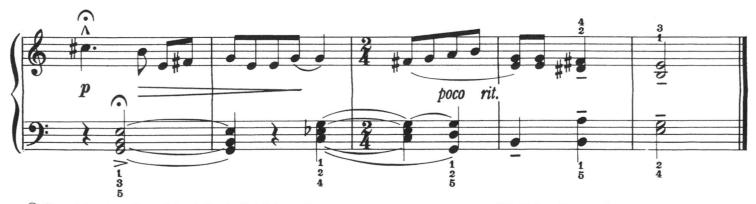

Three Hungarian Folk Songs

from "Beginners' Piano Music"

I.

Béla Bartók
(1881~1945)

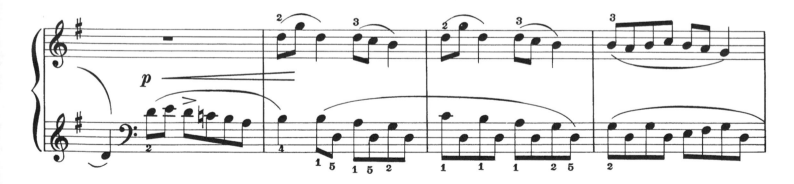

II.

Moderato

III.

Allegro moderato

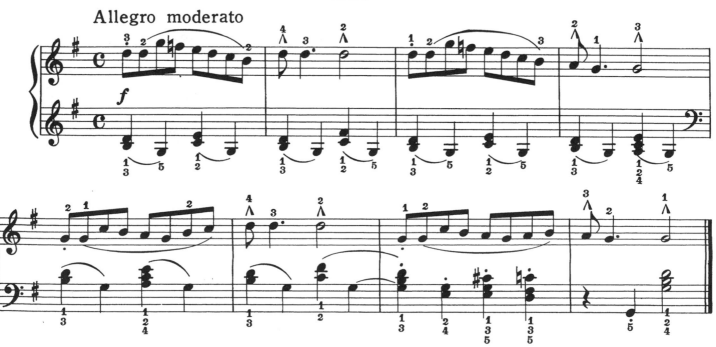

Peasant Song

From "Ten Easy Pieces"

Béla Bartók
(1881~1945)

Allegro moderato

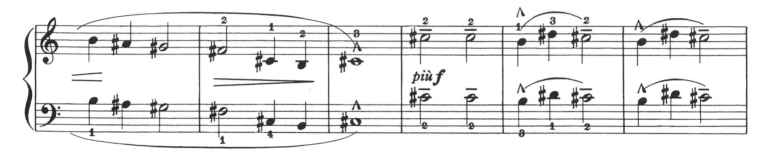

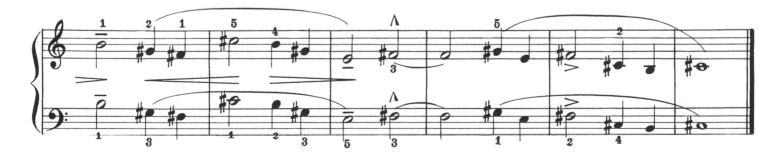

Two Pieces from "Guia Prático" N. 8

1. Poor Blind Woman
(Pobre Cega)

Heitor Villa-Lobos
(1881~1959)

2. Fly, Little Bird

(Xo! Passarinho!)

Heitor Villa-Lobos
(1881~1959)